Honey Doll

The Little Girl Who Would Become a Princess

Ruby Hall

With Addl. Memories by Diane Dunn

HONEY DOLL, THE LITTLE GIRL WHO WOULD BECOME A
PRINCESS, Ruby Hall and Diane Dunn

1st Ed.

◉◉◉ THREE SKILLET
www.ThreeSkilletPublishing.com

Edited by Farley Dunn
Cover Design by Farley Dunn

ISBN: 978-1-943189-26-7

$\mathcal{N}$ever was any child more wanted or more loved than *Honey Doll* . . .

You were so tiny, 5 lbs. 5 oz. and 18 inches long. I told the nurse to bring you over and let me touch you. The doctor said, "I'm sure glad you want this baby."

He didn't know how much!!

— *Ruby Hall* —

— *Part One* —

Germany

— *Part Two* —

The New Baby

— *Part Three* —

Honey Doll Turns Two

— *Part Four* —

Becoming a Princess

— *Part One* —

Germany

Chapter One

Dad, Barbara, and I arrived in Germany May 8, 1955, on Mother's Day. What a lonesome day that was, to look out of the hotel window and not be able to read any of the signs. We left Frankfort for Mainz, Germany. After being there for a while, I began to have problems with my health. The doctors said it would not get better by itself. They said I would have to have surgery, and then I wouldn't be able to have children. So we decided to have another baby, and then it wouldn't be so bad. After much morning sickness all day long and two or three visits to the hospital for glucose and rest, I went to Wiesbaden at the Air Force hospital. The next morning we had a baby boy and I was so thrilled. You see, I was wanting a boy, and Daddy wanted a girl. Afterwards, he was glad to have a boy. He had told my mother if it was a boy, she could have it. But he was quick to cancel that. In fact, after we came home, you would never have known he wanted anything except a boy.

———————————

My dad served 2 tours in Germany, one before I was born and one after I arrived. They were married in Fort Worth 7 years earlier. They were 21 and 22. In an early picture, probably taken on their wedding day, they stand side by side. My father grins like a Cheshire cat, and my mother looks as if she can't contain her happiness.

Mainz, Germany, in 1955 was the head-quarters for the American contingent monitoring the Allied rebuilding of Germany. WWII had ended only a decade earlier, and war damage still permeated the people's lives. My father played an important part in bringing new life to the city.

When they arrived, Mom was totally unprepared. She dealt with bouts of loneliness, and one morning, the apartment was cold. She snuggled with my sister Barbara to keep warm.

My sister, a toddler, was my mother's best friend during this time. My dad was away every day, the Germans spoke in German, and when the weather was too bad to go out, Mom and Barb played games to pass the time. I suppose, if one child was good company, how much better would two be?

Hospitals in Germany in 1956 weren't what we expect in America today. The Air Force hospital was a sterile place with little decoration, and too many people in too few rooms. However, the staff were courteous, even warm and friendly on occasion, and my mother's memories of her stay there are of the faces that smiled at her most often.

David was born in Germany, and the Germans didn't think my mother should take him out in public, that she should leave him home with a sitter. My mother tells the story of a German woman she met at the market that was appalled at seeing my brother, just weeks old, wrapped in a blanket and in his stroller going down the street. To my mom, it was a moment to be proud of, her new son on display.

How differently minds across the world seem to think!

Chapter Two

We took David and Barbara to the park when David was only a couple of weeks old. This was the huge park in Frankfort. Everyone was saying, oh, how small he was. They all thought he was so sweet (and so did we).

David was born 4:53 A.M., May 8, 1956, on a Tuesday, and we came home on Friday. On Sunday we couldn't wait to show him off, so we took him to church. We started him out right, real soon.

Growing up, church attendance was the most important event of the week. I should say events, because we usually went two or even three times.

Mom loves being at church, and she wants everyone to look their best when they walk through the door. Our family was always the best-dressed on the pew. You see, my mother was a seamstress, and a good one, too. I had new dresses, from frilly pink things with puffy skirts to color-blocked outfits directly from Saks Fifth Avenue. My brother and father were polished in new suits, as nice as any from a department store. (Of course, Saks was very much my mother's old brown Pfaff sewing machine.)

I'm sure my brother was all dolled up that May Sunday in 1956, with little booties, a hat on his head, and a matching jumper to ward off any chill that might try to seep inside and make him cry.

Mom worked in a pants-making factory after she was married, but before my sister was born. She and her good friend Emma went to apply, and Mom immediately qualified for an office job. Emma didn't, so Mom said she wanted to work in the factory, instead.

Mom learned so quickly, she was allowed to take every Thursday off and come back on Friday to get her paycheck. Her boss told her she was one of his favorite employees, and she earned a really good Christmas bonus that year.

I think she disappointed the people in the office,

because they hoped she would work in there. I'm glad, however, because I had new clothes to wear to church the whole time I was growing up. Everyone thought we were rich, we were so well dressed.

Thanks, Mom. I loved every new dress I ever wore, and I felt like a princess in every one. I couldn't ask for better memories of Sunday mornings, ever.

Chapter Three

Aunt Faye said she couldn't believe we had a boy until she saw him. So, I took his picture in his birthday suit and sent it to her. I told her to tear it up. However, after we came home, I was looking through her pictures and ran across it, so I took it out of the book and tore it up. I think he's glad I did.

Oh, my wonderful Aunt Faye! My Uncle Clarence always wanted a son, but he liked to joke that the only way there'd ever be any young men in their family was to marry one of his daughters off.

One picture of my brother as a toddler shows him wearing a full set of military greens, including a hat and his name stitched on his pocket. My mother sewed it by hand, with cuffs, regulation buttons, and even epaulets, just like his daddy wore.

Why did my mom really send that picture? For fun, probably, as much as anything. She was excited to have a new baby boy, and she wanted to share him with the world.

She did, too, even when her German neighbors frowned at her. It may have been Germany, and the year may have been 1956, but love was love, and my mother wasn't hiding my brother where no one could admire him.

I think she's still like that, eager to share what she's enthused about. If she gets a new house, she wants you to come spend the night. A new car? You're welcome to take a ride. Clothes, furniture, or even a new dish she's just learned to cook, she shares freely and without anything in return.

That's my mother's loving nature. I hope I got some of it from her, and that I'm willing to share God's blessings with my family and friends. I try, I really do. I'm not sure I'll ever match the example she's given me, even if I live to 103.

Chapter Four

One day I closed the door to our apartment and couldn't get back in without a key. David was in his crib and started crying. A friend tried to get a window open, but they were all closed, also. We called the M.P.s to unlock it. When they finally arrived, they had the wrong key. So we had to wait longer, and he had cried himself to sleep by the time they got the door open. You can imagine my relief to find him o.k.

One time we were in Leonard's Department Store in downtown Ft. Worth near the escalator. With three children, I'm sure it was difficult to get through the mass of shoppers and corral us all on the elevator at the same time. I was only a baby, but as I understand it, my mother pushed my stroller onto the escalator just as my brother broke free to chase down a balloon drifting across the floor. Of course, she had to go after him, and I was already headed up the escalator. At the end, we were all safe, but can you imagine the confusion, a baby on a trip alone up the escalator?

My son Steven, at three, once closed the bathroom door in our hotel suite, not realizing it would lock everyone out. I had just started the tub filling, and we panicked. Thank goodness maintenance arrived before the tub could overflow and flood the seven floors below us.

After locking my brother in the apartment, I'm certain my mother was desperate with fear. The awful thing for her was that everyone could hear the baby's cries, and then for the Military Police to arrive with the wrong key? My mom tells me that garage door openers are the best invention there is. She might forget her key, but she never forgets her car.

We laugh about near-disasters like this, are glad they're over, and file them away and forget about them. There's something more to this, however. When that door was finally unlocked, my mother didn't blame God for the locked door. Instead, she thanked him that my brother was safely asleep in his bed when she got inside.

My mother has a unique ability to trust in God in every situation. It's one of her best qualities, enabling her to find God's goodness in every situation. Little eyes learn what they see. From my mother, I've learned that God never lets us down, and we can trust him no matter what comes our way.

Chapter Five

And let's not forget how David used to cry and push his head against the rails in the bed. If I didn't get to him quickly enough, he would cry and push his head harder against the rails, until when I picked him up, he would have two ridges in his head. Oh, yes, and how he climbed out of the bed. I had it raised up higher so I could reach him easier. I didn't realize he could pull himself up. Poor Barbara got one spanking for pulling him out of the bed. She said, "I didn't do it. He did it." In a day or so as I was walking in the room, he was trying to come over the rail. I had to apologize to Barbara. Then I let the bed down some.

My sister was already a pint-sized grown up when my brother was born. Mom tells me that Barbara was all hers, and she wasn't sharing her with another. I think that means that Barbara had the run of the house, and she got to do just about anything she wanted, including boss my parents around from time to time. Of course, I'm sure my sister would disagree with that, but she was always the responsible one, taking care of things, a little mother in her own right. As I grew up, I remember her reading her Bible and praying, making sure she didn't do anything displeasing to God, and generally following my mother's example. Of course, Barbara, even at three, was indignant to be accused of pulling her baby brother out of his bed. I can hear her now, "No! I didn't do whatever you accused me of. If Jesus wouldn't do it, neither would I. How can you think that of me?"

I have no idea if David was capable of snickering at six months old, but somehow, that's how I picture him, his hand over his mouth, and his little baby chuckle, thinking, "That's a good one on you, Sis. And I bet Mom never finds out, either."

Except that my mother is pretty smart. There's not much that got past her when we were kids. Oh, we might fool her for a little bit, but she always saw through us in the end.

Mom's taught me something else. If you're wrong, always apologize. Never, never be the person who refuses to admit she's made a mistake.

I've made a few ill-thought-out accusations over the years, and the times I've followed my mother's example and asked forgiveness, it's made things right once again.

Then, I "let the bed down some more," or to say it differently, I change what I was doing so the misunderstanding doesn't happen again, and I get on with life.

I learned that from my mother. She was doing it before I was born, and she loves people in the same way, today.

Thanks, Mom.

Chapter Six

For a year or more Barbara and David tried to talk us into getting another baby. Anytime a friend of ours would have a baby, or a new baby would be in church, they would start all over again. Finally, I talked them out of the notion of wanting another baby. I told them how you would cry, and how I would have to spend so much time with you, and a lot of other things to discourage them. David started to school, and they were both kept pretty busy with school and everything; but there I was at home all by myself. Then I got to thinking how nice it would be to have another child. I talked it over with Daddy, and we decided we would put our order in.

Oh, oh, my brother and school! What stories his school walls could tell if they could speak to us now!

However, I wasn't born yet, and anything from this time period is hearsay only, so let me tell you of something I do remember.

My brother had a good friend named Ritchie. He was tall and thin, with short brown hair, and to my half-pint eyes, as handsome as any friend of my brother could possibly be.

I doted on him.

My brother took me everywhere, even when he was out with his friends. David's friends soon learned not to complain about me being along.

On one of these outings, it was David, Ritchie, Steve, and a fourth boy I don't recall. Steve hadn't wanted to come, because he knew my brother could be crazy. Steve sat in the back seat next to me. What I really recall about that outing was not where we went or what we did, but that my brother stood up for me. When Ritchie complained, David cracked to him, "Well, I can just pull over right now, and you can walk home."

Ritchie turned around from the front seat, put his arm up on the back, and he winked at me. Then he said, offhanded, as if anyone with any sense would say the same, "No, that's okay, man. That's cool."

Nothing else was said, but I think David would have done it, left Ritchie stranded on the side of the road, because I was more important to him.

I suppose I cried when I was a baby, and my mother probably had to devote more time to me than my brother and sister liked. I never knew anything about it. All I knew was how special I was, and that I was loved.

Thank you, Barbara. Thank you, David. I couldn't have had a better brother and sister than you.

Chapter Seven

After about three months or so, I went to the doctor for a check-up, and sure enough, they told me I was pregnant. I was so thrilled and excited I could hardly wait to tell Barbara and David, and of course, Daddy. I went to school to pick David up, and you can't imagine how excited he was. We went to pick Barbara up at Brownies, and David went running across the grass, and he could hardly wait to tell. He said, "Barbara, guess what! We are going to get a baby!" Then there were two so excited they didn't know what to do or who all they could tell. I told them to wait until after church. That way we could surprise everyone at one time. One of our neighbors went to our church, and I knew Barbara and David would want to be the ones to tell. Anyway, it wasn't long before everyone knew. But we really did surprise everyone at church on Easter Sunday. I wore a maternity dress. Some even asked if I was just wearing it, or was it for real. Sure enough, it was for real.

My brother's excitement reminds me of my husband and the birth of our son. I was blindingly excited at the idea of having a child of my own, but it was in the hospital when he was born that my husband's excitement first shown through. Just like David, running across the grass and yelling, "Guess what!" Farley was on the phone to everyone he knew to report the birth of his new son.

Then, and this is so very endearing to me, when we first took our son camping, Farley printed a banner that stretched across the front of the travel trailer, so that everyone in the campground would know we had a new baby on board. That was Farley's way of saying, "Guess what! We have a baby! He's healthy, beautiful, and ours!"

Our excitement over our son's birth was palpable, so I can understand my brother and sister's excitement over me. It's been over five decades since then. A lot of healthy babies have come into our lives. Barbara has three, David two (and grandchildren!), and there's my one. That's a lot of diapers to change.

Here's the important part of all this. Never has my mother shared anything but excitement at the births of her children. Even when we were at our worst, and we drove her to tears, she's always expressed her love for us.

I suspect she still feels that same surge of excitement every time she thinks of us swelling inside her with new life.

"Guess what, everyone! I've having a new baby! Don't you all want to come and see?"

My answer is the only one I can imagine. "Yes, Mom, of course I do. After all, that baby was me."

Chapter Eight

As usual, I asked God to bless me as I carried the
child He was giving us, and to form it just right,
and to use you for His glory.

Mom tells the most wonderful story from before she and my dad were married. It seems she was his Sunday school teacher. What I really think is that she was teaching him to fall in love with her. To hear her tell the story, she says he served in the Army in Trieste, Italy, and after returning to the U.S.A, he was sent to Korea in 1950. When he returned to the States in 1951 – and got out of the Army – my mother looked so beautiful to him, he simply had to propose.

She was horrified, to listen to her tell it.

Still, I think Mom was secretly pleased, even though she wasn't ready to get married at that point. She says she agreed for one reason. He lived a soldier's life, always here and gone again. He wouldn't change just because he was out of the Army, and once he was off again, he'd forget all about her. The fact was, he had already re-enlisted before he proposed.

I laugh about that now. After sixty-five years of marriage, did he forget? Not on your life. The funny thing was, in a way, my mother was partially correct. My dad wrangled his way out of his re-enlistment in order to marry my mother, but two years after they were married, my dad once again re-enlisted, and they were off traveling the world, just like Mom had predicted Daddy would do. Only this time, she was at his side.

I feel that's why I had such a happy upbringing. My parents set the finest example there could be, two young people, brought together by God, and even when my mom didn't think she needed to get married, God knew the perfect man was out to get her, and she couldn't be allowed to say no.

When my own son was born, my mother's prayers all those years ago came full circle. I was desperately sick with Steven, and yet he was born perfectly healthy. That was my mother's prayers from decades before still working their miracle in the life of the tiny daughter that had yet to see the first sunrise of her first new day.

Today, Steven is a grown man, he loves God with all his heart, and he listens to the Lord for direction in everything he does. I can only hope and pray that my prayers will inspire as powerful a legacy in Steven's children as my mother's have in me. I lift him in prayer regularly, following my mother's example, that God will use him in a mighty way.

Thank you, Mom, for your prayers, and for the example you set for me. The world is better because of you. You have a fine grandson to prove it.

— *Part Two* —

The New Baby

Chapter Nine

There was much sickness, and I went to the hospital
for glucose and rest. At about six months I had not
felt any movement, and the ones at church helped
me to pray about it. A nurse at church one night
was talking to me about my condition. She seemed
to think I was going to lose the baby, and she tried
to prepare me for it. I went home and cried. I told
Daddy but not the children. The next week I went to
the doctor and received a good report. I just wasn't
as far along as I thought. Oh, were we so happy!
Everyone rejoiced with us. Instead of October 4, the
doctor said it would be November 10. He only
missed it a day. How about that?

For years I heard about how sick my mother was
at the time, but I didn't really understand. Then,
when I carried Steven, I was hospitalized several
times. At one point, home health care came to the
house and tried to give me an IV to combat

dehydration, but my veins were too collapsed to accept the needles.

I thought my baby was dying, and I thought I was, too.

My doctor's advice was to eat and drink anything I could get down. I lived on Classic Coke and bean tacos for months, even as I lost over 50 pounds by the time my pregnancy reached full term.

The scariest moment of my pregnancy was during my first hospital visit. The doctor told me he would give me an ultrasound the next morning to see if my baby was still alive. That was one of the hardest nights of my life. I was so relieved the next morning to learn my baby was just fine.

My mom knew my dad for 5 years before they married. He visited her church, then would be gone a while, back to the church her father had built. I suspect my dad had caught her attention, even if she wouldn't admit to it. Mom says she prayed desperately not to leave her church for the little one her father had started. God said otherwise, and Mom began teaching the Sunday school class my father was in.

My grandparents had been praying my mother

would come to their church. My aunt Elsie played the piano and taught the children's Sunday school class. What better than to have two daughters helping together?

They didn't know their answered prayers would wind up with one of their daughters getting married.

Would my mother have done things differently if she'd known how sick she would be with me? Would she have refused to change churches if she'd been able to predict the fears she'd endure, that I might be born dead?

My mother became my strength, even as I struggled with my faith and endeavored to trust God that the magical life forming in my body still lived after months of worry and anguish.

Mothers to daughters, that's the best link in the whole world. I survived, Mom, because you survived. I appreciate you more than you can ever know.

Chapter Ten

*The church gave me a shower, and everyone gave
me girl things, because I said I was having a little
redheaded girl. Finally the day came, or rather, the
night. My mother had come to stay with us. Dad
and I went to the hospital about midnight. And
when Barb and Dave woke up, they heard the good
news of their new sister. Oh, what a happy day!*

When Mom was pregnant with Barbara, they
lived with my Dad's mother. Mom didn't feel
welcome there. They found someone in the neigh-
borhood who had a travel trailer and let them rent it
for $10 a month. Mom was growing bigger and big-
ger, and the little trailer didn't have a bathroom.
What a struggle that must have been!

Now, it's ten years later, I'm on the way, and

everyone's having a shower. How my mother's life had changed in only ten years!

One thing that hadn't changed was Germany. My sister was born in August of 1953, and my parents took her to Germany for three years. She spent her third birthday there.

I was born in the U.S. Army hospital at Fort Hood, between Copperas Cove and Killeen, Texas. How unexciting was that!

My parents didn't know they were to return to Germany in only a few years. That shower my mother loved so much was just a precursor to what the U.S. government had in store for my dad.

My father didn't care for Germany. He was unhappy after we arrived and wanted to be transferred home, but that wasn't happening. The Army didn't transfers lowly Sergeants just because they didn't like their assignments.

My mother's faith in bigger and better things through trust in God came into play, however, and my dad got just what he wanted.

My sister was babysitting for a couple, and the husband happened to be a Captain. He was able to get both him and my dad transferred out. God had a plan, but my parents didn't know it, yet.

We would rent a house on Bonzer Street in North Richland Hills, Texas, leave for Ohio for a couple of weeks, then move back to Fort Worth when Dad couldn't find work in Ohio.

Remember that plan of God's? It's like my brother and sister waking up to hear the good news they had a new baby sister. Oh, happy day!

My mother's faith was so strong that my family was about to have a happy day. And it would all be due to her belief in the power of a heavenly Father who can do anything his followers trust him for.

Chapter Eleven

You were so tiny, 5 lbs. 5 oz. and 18 inches long. I told the nurse to bring you over and let me touch you. The doctor said, "I'm sure glad you want this baby." He didn't know how much!!

I asked the nurse to make a footprint for me. She said since I had been so good, she could, but for me not to tell anyone, since they don't usually do that.

My mother always takes pleasure in the little things that others sometimes don't notice. My mother also doesn't mind asking for special favors, not because they are special, but because she is convinced people won't mind doing these extra things just for her.

Back when she was teaching my father's Sunday school class, at one point, she had about 20 students.

My Uncle Bo got saved, and then my Aunt Yvonne started coming to the church. (She wasn't my Aunt Yvonne until later.)

My mom says they never went anywhere except to church events. One time, my dad wanted to do something special for the family of the girl he wanted to marry. He took my mother's whole family out to eat, her parents and 8 brothers and sisters. He must have loved her a lot, because that was expensive.

Then, my mother tried on her sister Hazel's engagement ring. Mom says it was a mistake, because my dad saw her, took it as a hint, and he went out and bought my mother one almost like it.

My Uncle Clarence wasn't happy my dad was courting my mother. My grandparents weren't happy. None of my aunts and uncles approved. My mom wasn't happy getting that ring, either. Remember, she didn't want to get married.

The important thing was, God approved, and he's the one that counts, not the brothers and sisters, nor the parents of the bride.

If my mom hadn't put on that ring, who knows who my parents might have been. That little footprint that nurse made in that hospital room in Fort Hood, Texas, might have belonged to some other little girl. It didn't though, all because my mother asked her sister to let her wear her engagement ring.

I'm really glad my mother likes to ask little favors of others. Thanks, Mom, for being you.

Chapter Twelve

When the day came to bring you home, I took a shower before breakfast so I would be ready to go home as soon as I could. But the doctor said, since when you nursed, around your mouth would turn dark, he wanted to check you closer for heart defects. He told me to go on home, and I could pick you up tomorrow. "Oh, no," I said. "She is a breast baby, and I have to stay." He said o.k. The next day we took you home, and everything was all right. You weighed 4 lbs. 15 oz. then.

Barbara and David never got home so fast. I can imagine how long that day must have been for them. We took pictures of everyone holding you. Grandmother even had a turn. You were so tiny and oh, so sweet. I called you my "little angel" and sure enough, that is what you have been.

The day Steven was born, my room was swamped with visitors. It seemed everyone was there. The next day, you came and spent the entire day with me. Only one other visitor showed up. We spent our time holding my tiny new bundle of joy and going down memory lane, and it seemed the hours melted away.

Later that evening, Dad got off from General Dynamics, and he stopped by to see Steven and take you home. Another 50 visitors showed up after that, but we'd had the entire day together, you, me, and Steven. I never enjoyed time with you so much as that day.

When I was born, you had to stay an extra night because I wasn't ready to come home. When Steven was born, I had to stay at the hospital three days, because I'd been so sick while carrying him. I suspect you thought your extra time there was a burden. I was relieved to have a few more nights to rest and regain some of my strength.

I remember you telling me about how you were your daddy's little girl, and when you married Daddy, no one in your family approved. Your father said, "Well, if she's going to go ahead, there's nothing I can do about it. In six months, she'll be sorry and wanting out of it."

In six months, you were still married. Six years later, you were still together. Now, it's been over sixty years.

Was your father ever wrong!

I think a good marriage is like your love for your children. You love them in six months, and still in six years, and even sixty years later, you love them as much as ever. You and Daddy still tell me you love me every day. I'm glad I was your little angel all those years ago, and you still make me feel like one today. I feel loved, and I love you so much in return that I would burst if I tried to let it all out at once.

Chapter Thirteen

We went to Ft. Worth to spend the weekend when you were eleven days old. We just had to show you off. This was the day President Kennedy was assassinated. It was this week, and Daddy bought the movie camera. It seemed every time we would start to take your picture with the movie camera, you would hear the noise and get real still and look at us. Another trip to Ft. Worth was made at Christmas time. We stayed with Hazel and Carl.

———————————

Reading this, I realize we started Steven out the same way. He was three days old, and we had him out camping in the travel trailer. It was at Mineral Wells State Park. We only stayed the one night, but we had central heat, running hot and cold water, and an indoor bath with a sink, toilet, and tub. What a night that was, with a tiny tyke sharing the bed with us for the first time.

The best thing about that weekend was the quiet. The hospital had been a regular scurry of fun, bright with visitors in and out, and wonderfully enjoyable. What we needed, finally, was time alone just to hold our son and gaze into his face.

In that regard, our weekend was very different from yours. You had cameras, family to visit, and the death of a president on your hands. We had nature surrounding us and a warm furnace to ward off the chill of the night.

Then we picked up the pace, two weeks later heading to Memphis, Tennessee, to see "Mimi" Bonnie and "PaPoo" Jim Kahn. Only months later, Steven and I were off to New Hampshire with "Mawmaw" Sue and "Auntie" Malania to see Uncle Lee and Aunt Lili Ellison.

Steven didn't slow down then, because later that summer, we returned to New England, this time to Vinalhaven Island, to spend a week on Crockett's Point. Then came Canada, and Steven hasn't slowed down since.

I've never questioned where my roaming bug came from. You've always said my middle name was "Go." I think that might be Steven's middle name, also.

Steven "Go" Dunn. Yeah, we can say he comes by it honestly. He got it from you. And me. And PawPaw.

I wouldn't have him any other way.

Chapter Fourteen

David's Sunday school teacher gave him a little Chihuahua dog, and it was so tiny. You would crawl all over the floor with it.

At your first Christmas, I remember David and myself taking movie pictures of you on the couch beside a paper Santa Claus. For Christmas, you got a little red and white elephant with a wind-up in it, and a little pink elephant, and I don't remember all else.

———————————

I still remember that little Chihuahua. Or perhaps it's the movie film I've watched so many times that I picture in my mind, where that little dog chases me around, bouncing and play-nipping at my hands. I must have seemed more like that wind-up elephant than a real person to him. After all, people walk on two feet, talk in intelligible sentences, and wear something besides diapers.

Not me. I moved my arms and legs back and forth, just like a wind-up toy.

I kept that red and white elephant for over fifty years. Wow! Some of the things we hold on to. Some of the *memories* we hold on to. For example, I remember how clean you always kept our house. And wood floors. We had the shiniest ones around, so glossy I could see my reflection in them. In my memories I picture you cleaning all the time, and our house was always spotless and shiny.

I may have been a few years older to remember this, but in my mind, you were always cooking. You seemed to really enjoy it, and everything you pre-pared was so good! Sometimes you would even let me help you cook and clean.

Do you remember that pink bedspread and those pillowcases you made in pink Holly Hobbie fabric? You even sewed me curtains to match. I felt so special that you did that for me. My bedroom was so beautiful, more than anyone else's could ever be, thanks to my mom.

I never considered when we vacationed in Arkansas or Colorado that you cooked constantly while we were there. You never complained, and so I thought you were on vacation, too.

It wasn't much of a vacation for you, was it, Mom? I love you so very much. Thank you for all you've done for your family and for me. I'm aware of what you've given up for us, and I appreciate it more than you can know.

Chapter Fifteen

We were so excited when your teeth came in, and we thought you would never get any hair.

When you first took a step or two, we were again in Ft. Worth at Willis's in front on the sidewalk, and again we had the movie camera.

Oh, yes, and at Easter, I made you and Barbara pink and white dresses something alike. All three of you looked so good to me for church.

Holidays, holidays! How could holidays *not* have been important to you? You were married on the strangest one of the year.

When Daddy re-enlisted in the Army and proposed to you, I'll bet you were surprised. After all, he'd given you a slip for your birthday. It was underwear that his mother and some others of his relatives had picked out. I'll bet you were embarrassed. He also gave you a beautiful blue chenille bedspread his father had picked out, a substantial improvement over the slip.

That ring, though, remember? The one like Aunt Hazel's? You took it, said it was pretty, but you never, never admitted anything about it being an engagement ring. After all, you weren't getting married, not that day, and not that year. You hoped Daddy would be redeployed, and that would be that. He'd forget about you, and you could forget about him.

Then he talked the Army out of his re-enlistment. Whew, but I bet that surprised you! I know what really got your attention, though. It was when Grandmother came up to him, said we sure do miss our girls, and Daddy replied, "I sure do."

I'll bet you thought Daddy was crazy to say that. Grandmother was certainly nice to him while you stayed at Aunt Evelyn's. I bet Grandmother saw it coming, even if you didn't.

Then you asked if you could call Daddy, and Aunt Evelyn said you could. You told him you loved him, and that's when Daddy just couldn't wait any longer. He wanted to get married the next week, and you said it had to be on a Saturday.

It turned out to be Halloween. You wanted to change the date, and Daddy was afraid you'd change your mind. The wedding went on as planned, and that holiday was memorialized in a way no one would ever think possible, my parent's wedding anniversary.

I think you two are the reason I love holidays so much. I want to celebrate every one.

Happy Halloween! Happy Anniversary! Why not? In our family, they are one and the same.

Chapter Sixteen

*For your first birthday, as we took pictures of you
blowing out your candles, we said, "It's hot," and
you repeated, "Hot."*

After Christmas, birthdays are still the most
special events anyone can celebrate. I watched this
scene, with me blowing out the candles, on our
movie film so many times that I suppose I'd begun
to think this is how all lives start out, with candles
and cake.

After all, what could be better than being in the
spotlight with a lot of sweet stuff to smear all over
your face? Maybe it's why I love birthdays so much.

I never realized not everyone feels this way.
When Farley turned 40, I decided he needed a really

big birthday. I invited everyone we knew, including the people he worked with. There must have been a hundred people that showed up, and everyone seemed to have a wonderful time.

Afterwards, Farley said the next time he wouldn't come, even if it was his own party.

So, I began planning parties for Steven, instead. One year we were at the Oak Harbor beach. We had games and cake and sodas. The kids seemed to have fun, and I think most of the parents did, too. On a different year we held it in our back yard and driveway. Farley had to rebuild the gate that year so the kids could come in and out. Another year we were at Chuck-E-Cheese. That was the best birth-day ever. I didn't have to clean a thing!

I think everyone overlooks the real reason I'm so good at birthdays. I remember back to that first one, and I don't envision it the way it appears on that movie film. The celluloid version shows you guys telling me, "It's hot," and I reply back, "Hot."

I think you simply didn't listen closely. I didn't say, "Hot." I said something else, entirely.

I'm only saying this once, so listen carefully this

time. What I said then was, "I'm hot," only you guys didn't know how to pay proper attention.

Oh, all right. I'll say it again.

"I'm hot, and don't you know it."

Love you, Mom. You've always treated me as though I'm special, and I've always believed you. I think that's what you intended, and it worked on me.

You're the best, Mom, and you always will be.

Chapter Seventeen

In October 1965, Daddy received orders for Germany, and my mother had come down to stay with us for a while. Barbara and David rode the train back to Ft. Worth with her. We were busy cleaning the house and getting everything ready to be packed, so Dad was at home a lot. One day you called him "honey." It sounded so cute, and you just started calling him that all the time. He said, "Okay, you call me Honey, and I'll call you Honey Doll." So that is how that nickname came about. It just seemed to stick, and everyone called you Honey Doll. In fact, you thought that was your name.

It seems we were always staying with one family or another when I was little. I remember some of it, although I suppose a portion of my memories come from Mom and Dad, as I wasn't around at the time.

The one of Juanita and Roy seems sad to me. Roy was just home from prison camp. He and Juanita had a military apartment with several bedrooms, and Mom and Barbara would stay with them. It had stairs and a landing, and one day, Barbara came out of the bathroom and tumbled down the stairs. Although I don't think my sister was hurt, a neighbor had to calm Mother down, she was so upset.

My sister took off for the Philippines when I was about nine, to live with some of our missionary friends. See what I mean? Our family was always off to stay with whoever would have us. We thought nothing of it, because we were a wandering family. Anyway, Barbara would have been college age then, an adult both legally and because she was so much more mature than most girls that age. I wrote her a couple of times a week and was excited every time we heard from her. I always pictured her there praying and doing the Lord's work. Now I suspect she managed to have a good time, too, not *always* reading her Bible and on her knees. It's funny how I thought that's all she did over there.

I don't know if my sister's trip to the Philippines inspired you and Daddy to take off to India when I was 18, or if you would have gone anyway simply because you were ready to be off once again. Do you remember how disappointed we were when our sponsoring Indian pastor hadn't set anything up, and we were shipped off to the tip of the subcontinent where no one spoke English? I do, because I got really sick. I remember you praying into the night for me to be well, and for God to protect our family.

During that terrible time in India, my one bright spot was Daddy calling me Honey Doll. That name was a bit of home, and I felt loved when he called me that, even if I didn't love being on the opposite side of the world from where I really wanted to be.

Thanks, Mom, for letting me steal a little of your "honey" from your honey. Sharing is what you do best, and I'm glad you shared Daddy with me.

— *Part Three* —

Honey Doll Turns Two

Chapter Eighteen

We were at Mom's about two or three weeks before
we left for Germany. Your second birthday was
celebrated there with cake and ice cream. We got
you a beautiful blue and white snowsuit and some
little toys.

———————————

Was that the snowsuit that was left on the airplane when we flew to Germany? I don't suppose I
could have worn it long, but you must have been
very disappointed to have it gone before I got to put
it to good use.

This must have been the trip that we lived in the
first floor apartment. Barbara was a climber, and
you were afraid she'd push the screen out and tumble to the ground if we were on the third floor. She
might have, too, but as I recall, she survived her

tumble down the stairs in Juanita's apartment. Barbara was tough. Nothing seemed to slow her down.

I don't know if you ever knew about the motorcycle race. I was about ten, then, and I was on the back of David's bike. We were on Northeast Loop 820, and we saw Barbara in her car. They started racing, and when David leaned forward into the handlebars, the wind caught me and pushed me onto the taillight. I was holding on with my fingertips when Barbara saw me and slammed her brakes, pulling to the side of the road.

I was crying and shaking, and David had no idea why Barbara had pulled off the road. He did apologize, over and over. I knew he didn't mean for that to happen, and just like the worshipful little sister I was at that time, by the end of the week, I was back on the motorcycle with him again. I think we must have had an unspoken agreement not to tell you and Dad that your oldest two children very nearly killed your very favorite daughter. I never said anything, anyway, not that I can remember.

Would you have restricted David's motorcycle if you'd known? Or how about Barbara's car? It's like that snowsuit. Would you have given me something else if you'd known it would be lost on the airplane? What I think is that you felt so much joy in giving us gifts, that the consequences of those gifts were part of it all. You gave us Germany, Hawaii, India, that big gold Buick Electra, Barbara's Mustang, David's bike, and so much love that we felt protected and safe, even when we pushed the limits of what we were allowed to do.

That's good parenting, when your children feel secure in life. I'm glad I grew up with a mother as wise and smart as you.

Chapter Nineteen

We arrived at Joe and Rosetta's Thanksgiving night and spent a few days with them before going to New Jersey. We flew over to Frankfurt and spent the night there. We left on a big bus the next morning for Munich, Germany.

———————————————

Remember Uncle Jody's little church? You and Aunt Elsie used to attend there. I was always afraid for you, because I didn't think it was a good part of town, but I know better now. It's not the part of town where you build your church; what matters is the power of God that you have in your heart. God keeps us and protects us when we trust in him. I've learned that from you over the years.

It seems the men in our family have always been building churches to draw the lost to God.

Uncle Clarence has built several, some for other ministers, but his on Baker Boulevard, especially. It's been there over 20 years, and it's still as beautiful as ever. Clarence and Faye invited Farley and me there frequently, but it was so far from our house in Azle. Still, we drove over for special occasions, weddings and other celebrations. We had such nice fellowship in the big room at the back, with the kitchen and tablecloths on all the tables.

On that flight to Germany, I can hardly imagine you with three children to corral, and me so small. What was I, about two? I remember a little about that trip, but mostly about it taking a long time, and after a while, I learned that being on an airplane wasn't fun. You've always said that Barbara and David were like a little mommy and daddy to me. Actually, you said Barbara and David thought I was wonderful, and you could see David adored me. I hope on that trip they played with me a lot and let you take a nap. You probably needed it.

I think I remember a little about the snow after we got there. There wasn't any, and then there was. Maybe that's why snow is so special to me, and it always has been. Haven't you said we visited the Black Forest while I was in Germany? See, from the time I was a baby, you and Daddy made my life a fairy tale. I was a princess in a snow-covered castle, and I spent my free time exploring the Black Forest, protected by powerful Queen Barbara and the valiant knight, Sir David.

I was the luckiest little girl alive, with the best parents in the world.

Chapter Twenty

Everyone there loved you, because we all loved you so much, and they all called you Honey Doll. There was a teenage boy who lived upstairs named Gary Wells. You would reach out the window if he was outside and say, "Touch me. Touch me, Gary." He would always stop and talk to you.

You had a little scooter to ride, and one lady who lived above us let you play with her boy's tricycle. Oh, yes! You loved wearing high heels to play in. You would clomp, clomp down our hallway, and the lady upstairs said she couldn't figure out what it was. I know she didn't appreciate it. Ha, ha.

I actually remember Gary, believe it or not. I don't know what interested me about him, but I'd wiggle my fingers when I called to him. He probably reminded me of David, or maybe it was just the attention. As you know, I enjoy getting a lot of that!

I can imagine wearing those high heels and the tall spikes going tap, tap, tap. I liked the sound as much as anything and had no idea someone else might be irritated by it. I wonder how many scratches I put in your polished floors?!? I was having fun, and that's all that mattered to me.

Do you remember the bright pink pair of heels I talked you into buying for yourself? I suppose I was five, then. They were the prettiest shoes I'd ever seen. You wore them to church, and I felt fancy when I walked in beside you. I don't remember what happened to those shoes, worn out and tossed away, I guess. They were fun, weren't they?

My scooter reminds me of Steven's red car. He drove it everywhere. His was electric, so much better than using your feet. We used to attach his green wagon, and he pulled it all over the yard, sometimes with passengers riding along. (People, occasionally, and other times, animals, stuffed or real.)

I loved it that you never minded Steven being a little boy, with all the noises, mess, and attention that swirled all about him. His best times were with you and Daddy traveling in the truck, delivering cars across the country. Even then, Steven was your favored helper, never a hindrance.

That's how I felt growing up, always wanted, and never in the way. That's how all children should feel, loved and treasured for who they are. I appreciate you doing that for me.

Chapter Twenty-one

Dad had to leave for Berlin right after we got there, but God answered prayer and let him come home for Christmas. The ground was covered with snow, and we didn't have a car. After we found out they were having service on Saturday night, we walked over to the chapel.

I would push your stroller over in the snow to the post office to check the mail. After two or three weeks, we found out they had been sending our mail to a different place, so we went after it. How excited we were!

I remember that stroller you and I bought Steven at the Mall of America in Minnesota. It was green, had tons of storage, and best of all, it collapsed down with the touch of a lever. We used that stroller for years, even when Steven outgrew it, because it was like pushing a shopping buggy everywhere we went.

I think this mail mix-up is why you always get so excited when the mailman comes. In Germany, that was your lifeline to the world. Phone calls were prohibitively expensive, you didn't have the Internet, and you knew almost no one. The mail was the excitement of *what if*, the possibility that someone was thinking of you and sending you a letter or a card.

I get that from you. I imagine something special in the box each time I open it. I forget people mail bills, also, and they seem to surprise me every time. That's not so fun.

I can hardly imagine how difficult it was for you to leave your family to go to a foreign country, especially at Christmas. My first Christmas married to Farley, I broke down in tears, not because we didn't have a Christmas tree and decorations, but because it wasn't what I'd enjoyed all my life with you, Daddy, Barbara, and David. Christmas is a time for traditions. When they're broken, we feel lonely. Aren't you glad you had three children to keep you busy?

I remember your story about being so homesick

that Daddy promised you that you could call home, even though it was very expensive. When you got the operator, she said you had to be on a waiting list to make an overseas call. You said that by then, you wouldn't be homesick any longer, so never mind. How funny you much have sounded to the operator!

Not only did Dad sacrifice a lot for his country and family, but you also sacrificed. Thank you both so much for your sacrifices you made over the years. I love and appreciate you both so much!

Chapter Twenty-two

When Dad came home we would go to Garmish [sic] to the mountains.

I took you with me to the museum with Barbara's school class. Again, as usual, you got a lot of attention from them all.

We spent the summer watching David play baseball.

I think Mother's love for museums, school events, and sports came from her early years in her church. She and my father were in the same Sunday school at Bro. Michener's church. Of course, that meant she was around a lot of people, and Mom loves being with people. Then her father started a church service for the seniors on Tuesday night, because he felt sorry that they didn't have the opportunity to take a real part in the church services on Sunday. The sad thing is, that's what prompted him to build his own church. There was a misunderstanding, and he felt he had to move on. He didn't want to preach, so he was only the Sunday school superintendent in the new church, but it was established by him. It was Bro. Michener who encouraged my mother to change churches to attend with my father, assuring her the church would miss her. He understood that when the Lord speaks to us, we have to do what he says.

Mom's love for museums must have rubbed off on Barbara. Growing up, it seemed as though she took me constantly, just the two of us. My big sister was the best kind of sister, making things fun for me, and never minding that I was tagging along. I felt like she enjoyed spending time with me.

At one of David's baseball games when I was older, he was pitching, and I remember shouting, "Atta boy, David! You can do it!" Everyone looked at me like I was crazy, but I didn't care. That was my brother out there. Then, after the game, I got to run around the bases. It could have been a Texas Rangers game, and it wouldn't have been any more special to me.

As far as me getting a lot of attention, well, we all know how that goes. I never felt left out, and that's the important thing. Family mattered, and I felt I mattered most of all.

Chapter Twenty-three

In July 1966, we received orders to come back to Ft. Hood. We were happy about that. So in August, we left Germany to come home. We stopped by Ohio to try to settle there, but after Dad got back to Texas, he wanted us to come home, also. He had to make another trip to Ohio.

We found a house across the street from Hazel. We lived on Bonzer Street. If anyone asked where you lived, you would say B on Bonzer. I really don't know why.

I remember the stories of why Dad was so glad to get home from Germany that second time. He likes things orderly and structured, and he felt everyone in the military should be the same. Rules were rules, and you didn't try to break them. The people he was around in Germany didn't feel the same. They felt free to say, "I don't like this," or, "I don't want to do that." That wasn't my father's style. That's when he got together with a Captain on base, and together they got transferred out of there.

I remember the stories of Uncle Jody and Aunt Rosetta living in Ohio. Stopping by on the way home from Germany didn't make an impression on me, but now I'm certain I had jetlag, even as young as I was. I know Grandmother was living with them then, and after we got back to Fort Worth, Uncle Clarence went to Ohio to pick her up, and she lived with us. I used to say to her, "Grandmother, have you taken your pill? Take your pill, Grandmother."

Either she thought I was darling and cute, or I really irritated her. I only have positive feelings, however, so I guess it was all right.

What really sticks out in my mind is moving into our house on Bonzer Street. I was very insistent that it was "B on Bonzer." I think I got that from mother, because some people thought she was saying Donzer. She would say, "It's B on Bonzer," and from that time on, I knew where I lived. My street was called "B on Bonzer," and no one could tell me any different. After I married, I had Farley drive by the old house to show it to him. In my childhood eyes, it was the best house in the world, and I loved it. My adult eyes revealed the truth. It was the perfect home for a family without a real income, and I can understand why you and Daddy were so glad to get our brand new apartment on Belknap Street the next year.

Still, B on Bonzer fills me with fun memories, and I wouldn't trade a one.

Chapter Twenty-four

Clarence went to Ohio in December to get Grandmother, and she moved in with us after she got sick and had to take medication. You would always want to give her a pill. You also gave her love.

———————————

I wish I could have recorded the stories Grandmother Huffman used to tell me. What would they sound like now? Cows getting their heads stuck in fences, little boys playing mischief on their school friends, or little girls in pink dresses, with all their dreams coming true.

Those stories are gone and mostly forgotten. So, when Steven was small, we used a recorder to tape many of his bedtime stories. Farley's in the process of compiling them into a book, so that Steven can retell the stories to his own children one day.

I had forgotten about Grandmother insisting I get her medication for her. I'm glad I was smart enough to remember that you'd already given it to her. This must have been the reason I asked her repeatedly to remember her pill.

Grandmother shared my room with me. I didn't mind. I thought all lucky little girls got to have their grandmothers live with them. She loved on me, even when she felt bad, so I know she must have really loved me. When she went to the hospital, she stayed for several weeks, but she never came home. I enjoyed having my grandmother share her life with me.

My mother tells this story of when she was seven, just a few years older than I was when Grandmother Huffman came to share my room. That was when my mother got saved. She knew all the Bible stories. The Hartfield boys from Dallas came over and held a revival. Before every service, they held children's church. The leader would bring 3 candy bars with him, and after the story, the three children who answered his questions best got the candy bars. My mother always got the first one.

I'm convinced to this day this is the reason Mom adores chocolate so much. As a little girl, I was interested in Grandmother Huffman, holding my own church services with my stuffed animals, and being a good little girl.

Like mother, like daughter. We become the people around us, and I grew up okay, because I'm like you (except for your love of chocolate, of course).

Chapter Twenty-five

A house down the street became vacant, and we wanted to get it. You began telling everyone we were going to move there. Then we found it was already rented, but you kept saying, "We are going to move in there." Hazel would say, "No, Diane. It is already rented." You would say, "We are going to move there." And sure enough, we did. How about that?

I remember how everyone thought I was silly for saying we were moving to that house. It was obvious to me, and I was frustrated that no one else could see it. I think it was like when you were in Germany before David was born. You were having problems with your health, and they wouldn't go away. You were told you weren't having any more children. Most people would have given up and said, "Oh, well. We have a healthy girl, so one's enough."

Not you and Daddy. You said, "Let's have another while we still can." If you hadn't said that, where would that leave me? Not born, that's for certain.

I've watched you do this over and over, see things you want that other people say you'll never have, and suddenly they're yours. We got our washing machine at the Topper Court house that way. One day, you said, "Diane, we can have a new washer and dryer. Let's go get them." After that, we didn't have to go to the laundromat any longer. That was an exciting day for me, and now that I'm grown, I understand how special it was for you.

You and Daddy have bought cars and houses that way, also. You drove your new blue Buick, and you had the white van that was so nice inside. What about the Richardson house? You never thought you could live in such a nice place, until Daddy came home and said it was ours.

Your confidence is your faith in God bleeding into everything you do. You know he wants the best for your life, and you trust him that what he wants is what you want, also. Then you claim it, and it becomes yours.

I also remember how you told people you were having a redheaded baby girl when I was born. What happened there? I don't have a red hair on my body anywhere.

Love you, Mom.

Chapter Twenty-six

Another thing that was funny. They were building a new building on Grapevine Hwy, and there were no signs as to what it was. You said it was a money building. We said, "What do you mean, a money building?" You said, "You know, a place where you get money." And were we surprised when they put up a sign of a finance company. You were just too smart.

I remember something else, too. The same thing happened when they built Zyder Zee Fish Restaurant on Grapevine Hwy. I told everyone it was going to be a fish place and no one believed me.

While I was growing up, I remember driving all the way across Fort Worth to Seminary South Mall and downtown to Leonard's Department Store. There was construction everywhere. North Richland

Hills was booming. Then they built North Hills Mall on Grapevine Highway, although it's been torn down since. For a while, it was a good place to shop. Northeast Mall kept getting larger. And the houses, they sprouted up on every street, for miles and miles.

The biggest change I remember from my childhood to adulthood is Colleyville. Remember how tiny it was, and when we visited at Colleyville Assembly, it was out in the middle of nowhere? Now, you can hardly find the church because the city is so huge around it.

Then there's Rufe Snow Drive. It was two lanes, one each way. The big bridge over Loop 820 went in first, and the first half mile of Rufe Snow wended northward with four lanes and a turning lane in between before turning back into a two lane road. By the time we bought the house on Richardson, Rufe Snow was six lanes, three each way.

I cringe when I think about the years they spent on the 820 interchange at Highway 121. You couldn't go anywhere without construction adding 20 minutes to your drive. No more was that finished, than it was time to tear up 820 to add more lanes of traffic.

In my mind, it all started with that finance building going up on Grapevine Highway. From there, North Richland Hills added a waterpark (NRH_2O), about a million houses, and restaurants everywhere.

What was better was the family I got during those years. Now Steven is an adult I'm very proud of, and I know you are, too.

Now, if they'll just build a money building that's all mine (the money part, at least), they can stop the construction at last. Until then, I say, "Build away!"

Chapter Twenty-seven

We enjoyed living right next door to Uncle Bo and Aunt Yvonne. You went over to visit quite a bit. We got you a swing set for your third birthday. You really liked it. Every time anyone came over, you would say, "Have you seen my new swing set?" After doing this so much, when Bo would see you, he would say, "Diane, have you seen my new swing set?"

Also, Bo would try to get you to say root beer, and son-a-gunny. You thought it was bad, so you would not repeat it. I suppose you thought beer was bad, and you wouldn't even say it. He would say, "I'll give you $10.00 if you say root beer." You just wouldn't say it for anything.

I'm still like that with words. To type the word beer makes my fingers feel dirty. When Steven was young, I taught him that stupid was a bad word. He doesn't like it to this day.

Years ago, Dick and Barbara bought a high-quality redwood swing set and slide combo for Richard and Charity. We later set it up in our yard. Steven played on it for years. I think I was as proud of it as he was. It had a raised platform on one side, and Farley added walls, with a round bubble window as tall as Steven. He attached a blue peaked roof overhead, and that platform became a fort for Steven and his daddy.

Farley's brother used to tease Steven when he was small. One day I got tired of it, and I put my foot down. After that, his brother never said another thing like that to tease Steven.

Uncle Bo and Aunt Yvonne weren't religious, and our family was very religious. I wasn't sure how to behave around people who didn't go to church and believe in Jesus. I was uncomfortable, even though I do remember being over there a lot. I wished Uncle Bo wouldn't try to make me say those things he wanted me to say. Now I know they weren't bad words, but they seemed that way to me then. I'm sure I stamped my feet at least once to get him to stop, but I was a little girl, and who listens to little girls except their mothers and fathers?

I used to pray for Uncle Bo and Aunt Yvonne at night. I don't know if they ever accepted the Lord, but I loved them anyway. I think they knew that, and they loved me back.

Chapter Twenty-eight

We all had so much fun with you. What a sense of humor you had, and oh, so witty. We couldn't believe some of the things you would say.

One time you were at Bo and Vonne's, and he started taking his shirt off. You said, "Oh, I had better go home, now."

———————————

I've always enjoyed fun things, so I like to make things fun for other people. It's your fault. You took us to Leonard's, remember? They had a children's department, with a mini-train and a mini-movie theater. I could ride that train around the ceiling, and I did, lots of times. The attendant at the theater would always give me a cookie or popcorn, and I'd get to watch cartoons while you looked through the merchandise.

That's where it all started.

I know this next memory wasn't meant to be funny, but I'm reminded of the time you took me to the Richland Plaza Shopping Center to let me practice my driving in the parking lot. I needed the entire parking lot, too, because our car was an aircraft carrier. Even today, how do people drive such large cars? At 17, I thought I was about to launch an F16 every time I hit the brakes or touched the gas. I could barely control it, and to park it? That was impossible.

I made a good choice when I went to take my driving test. My friend Tamra drove the smallest car in production at the time, a Ford Pinto. We went on my 18th birthday, and after your big car, Tamra's was like parking a roller skate, easy as could be. I don't suppose my test evaluator would have found it funny if I had sideswiped another car with him riding along. I was so nervous I would have done that in the aircraft carrier, I'm certain.

When I was out with David and his friends, I tried to be funny so they would like me. Sometimes I would do silly stuff, like stand on one leg, or make funny faces. When they laughed, I knew they didn't mind if I was along.

When we managed the ice cream shop, I found that if I smiled, I made more sales. People like people who like them; and if I'm enjoying life, then that carries over to the people I'm with. I think that with Uncle Bo, I didn't mean to be funny, but I'm glad it sounded that way. I'd hate to have hurt someone's feelings. I just didn't want to see a man without his shirt on. I thought it made sense to leave while he was still completely dressed.

Chapter Twenty-nine

*You were so sweet to Grandmother, to give her a
drink, and you always wanted to give her her
medicines (pills or aspirin), and you would talk to
her a lot.*

*And remember your rabbits the lady at church gave
you and David? It was so cute how they would eat
carrots out of our hands. How sad it was when the
weather was so hot, and they died.*

Grandmother and I talked all the time. I remember she was unable to walk, so it was funny when she tried teaching me how to make up my bed. It wasn't a large bed. In fact, I still slept in a baby bed. Making it was a challenge, because I was in it at the time! I tried, though, and eventually, I think we were successful to some degree.

The rabbits were fun to have. I named my favorite one "Twitchy" because of his whiskers. It was funny to see them wriggle as he sniffed of my hand. I liked to hold him when I got on my swing set, and we'd go back and forth. He seemed to enjoy all the attention. I guess it must have been a bad summer, with lots of sun and heat. One day, David came in and said the rabbits were dead. I didn't want to believe him, and it was a very sad day when Daddy loaded them up in the truck to take them to the dump. When he drove off I chased the truck down the street crying.

When I was a little older and had parakeets, and they passed away, you would help me package them up in tissue in a box. We had real funerals for them. Daddy would go out back with the box, and we would read the Bible and pray. I didn't feel as sad after that. What made the difference was that you cared about everything that concerned me. Even if it was just a bird, it meant something to me, and you took time out of your day to wrap your love around me.

When we moved to North Carolina, I had to face death all over again with Heather and Beckie, our dogs. They were too feeble to make the trip, and it was up to me to let them go easily. I held them in my arms at the vet's, and it was hard. Losing loved ones is always difficult, even when you know it's the best thing for them.

I still think of Grandmother from time to time. I remember Twitchy and my birds and the dogs I had to let go. What I remember even more is how much I loved them, and I can't ever regret how much love they gave back to me.

— *Part Four* —

Becoming a Princess

Chapter Thirty

Once when Dad was driving a truck out of town, you were laying in my bed, and we were talking. I began to tell you about heaven and how Jesus went back to heaven, and He said He would come again for us after He prepared mansions for us. You began to cry and say, "I don't want to go." You were afraid you were going to go right then. I explained we wouldn't go until we all went at the same time. You thought that was o.k. A few days later you were sitting at the back porch, and I heard you yelling, "Jesus, come get me! Jesus, come back and get me!" Then I had to say, "Lord, don't hear her cry right now."

Grandmother became very sick, and we had to take her to the hospital in June, 1967. She was there about two weeks, and she went on to be with Jesus. It was sad, but it was good. Her mission in life was finished. She went on to receive her reward.

———————————

There are times I lay on my bed to rest, and Steven comes in to talk. Sometimes we discuss topics that make a difference in the world, and other times, we talk about things that make a difference in our hearts. That's the time when we learn about each other, and we can share how we feel about God.

That day when you were talking to me all those years ago was the first time I remember heaven as a very real place. It was a quiet moment, where you shared how you believed, and I accepted your words to be truth. And they were, revealing life-changing truth to me.

That's why you caught me on the steps calling out, "Jesus, come and get me!" Then, when he didn't respond, I figured he hadn't heard me, so I yelled it louder.

Your words to me when you joined me on the steps gave me a deeper understanding of our relationship to God. You encouraged me not to yell those words, because one day, when it was time for me to go to heaven, Jesus would come to get me. I didn't have to ask him. He would do it, because he loved me and wanted me to someday go live with him.

Our discussion was in God's perfect timing, because one day not long after, you came home very sad. You explained to me that Grandmother wouldn't be coming home again. Jesus had come to get her, and she was in heaven with him.

I was happy for Grandmother, but I was sad for you. You missed Grandmother. I know now how much you suffered. It's hard to let loved ones go, even when you know they are with Jesus.

I'm fortunate to still have you. I thank the Lord every day.

Chapter Thirty-one

That following December we decided to move to Ohio, to be with Uncle Joe. We didn't stay but about a week. We rented a big two-story house with a basement. We even set up our Christmas tree (an aluminum one). Daddy couldn't find a job, so we decided to come home. We had spent the night with Clarence and Faye in their beautiful home in Diamond Oaks before we left. Faye said, "Ruby, if things don't work out, don't hesitate to come back." And sure enough, we did. We spent Christmas with them while trying to find another place to live.

We packed up a U-Haul with all our things. My strongest memory is that we went far, far away, and we drove for hours and hours to get there.

How could any place be so far away from the only home I really remembered? Ohio? What was that? Was it on the far side of the moon? Uncle Jody and Aunt Rosetta lived there, but I barely knew them at the time. Daddy couldn't find a job in Ohio, so even though we'd already moved into a house, within weeks, we'd packed up once again, ready to head back to Fort Worth.

It may have been only weeks spent in Ohio, but it seemed like a lifetime to a 4-year-old girl.

When I was first married, it was a similar feeling. I'd lived in North Richland Hills for as long as I remembered, and everything was within a couple of miles. Stores, restaurants, even my friends. In only minutes, I could be anywhere.

Then I moved to Azle. I was forever away from anyplace I wanted to go. If I needed a new pair of hose, it was a thirty-minute drive to the mall. Who wanted to live in Azle? Well, I did, because my husband was there, but I'd rather be back in civilization where the shops and restaurants were.

I think Ohio for my mother was the same. Her mother and brother were there, but she was half a continent away from most of what she knew. Who wanted to live in Ohio? What made her follow my dad across four states and back home again? One thing. Love. At four, I was about to experience a new sort of love. It would be a time I'd never forget.

We spent Christmas with my Uncle Clarence and Aunt Faye and my two cousins. Santa Claus came to see me, and my uncle's street was renamed Candy Cane Lane for the season. Cars drove by every night to see all the lights. That Christmas was fantastic!

Best of all, my family was there.

You taught me that, Mom. As long as you have your family with you, you have everything you need. You and Daddy, and Barbara and David, and of course, me. We were together, and that made this part of my life special, indeed.

Chapter Thirty-two

They had put our other house up for sale. We couldn't find anything that we could afford, so we called about it and asked them to let us rent it until they sold it. Praise the Lord, they said o.k. So we moved back in it. It was so very cold the day we moved in. I remember Barbara and David being so concerned for you. They wrapped you up in a blanket, and we got the hair dryer and plugged it in to blow warm air under the blanket.

While we were at Faye's, on Christmas Eve, you were upstairs, and we put your doll in the living room in a chair. When you came down, we said, "Diane, did you hear something a while ago? I think we heard Santa. Go see if he came." Sure enough, you went in and found your doll. You couldn't imagine how he had come in without anyone seeing him.

I was sitting with you when you called them

about the house. I didn't want to leave Uncle Clarence's, because Christmas had been so much fun there, but if we had to go, I wanted it to be to Bonzer Street. You were so excited when they said we could move in. Of course, we had to get the utilities turned on. Barbara carried me into the house, and David helped hold a blanket around me.

But that's putting the cart before the horse. That Christmas at Uncle Clarence's, I really did have a real Santa Claus come to see me. I didn't figure out for years that it was Dad. I should have noticed that Santa wore the same suit every year, and Santa was always the same size as my father. To my eyes, however, he was really the man in red, and I loved him as such.

I never could figure out how my doll got into that chair. It seemed to me that *someone* would have noticed. Yet, that only made it more magical. I never let go of it, and that's got to be the reason I still half expect to see Santa's burly red chest chuckling with laughter, and a "Ho, ho, ho," every Christmas season. I never gave up on my fascination with that mysterious doll sitting in that chair. It's like, if I look hard enough, I'll find him, because he's got to be real. He's just got to.

And he is.

Santa came back to visit with Steven when he was a boy. Yes, Santa still looked the same height and shape as my dad, and his voice sounded like PawPaw's, but he was real as real can be, even if he was just Dad once more when the suit made its way back its storage box.

Chapter Thirty-three

So we moved back into the house on Bonzer, and Dad went back to work at General Dynamics. We set your swing set up, and Barbara and David started back to school.

I'll bet you hoped David didn't do what he did the first time he started to school. Remember? He started asking for another baby, and you got me. Whoops!

I love that story, though, how when you got pregnant with me, David ran out the door and told all the neighbors that his mommy was going to have a baby.

I also like hearing you tell about taking me to church, how everyone was so excited to see the new baby. Everyone wanted to hold me, and Barbara got right up next to me and said, "No, you can't hold her."

You asked Barbara why, and she said, "She's ours."

At night, Daddy would put me into your bed so you could nurse me, but one night I frightened you. You dozed off, and when you woke up, I was gasping for breath.

You must have been really afraid I might die. You wanted to protect me, to keep me safe no matter what happened.

You still do that for me. And just like Barbara did with the people who wanted to hold me, I've said the same thing to people about Steven. No, he's all mine. It was difficult getting him here, and I don't want to share him with anyone.

We were all a family, and we were still together, but I was glad to see my swing set back up. As long as I had my swing set, I knew I was at home. I remember every time someone came over, the first thing I'd do was grab them by the hand and lead them outside to show off my swing set.

I also enjoyed my great big doll.

We settled in, and I felt at home on Bonzer Street. I didn't want to move ever again.

Chapter Thirty-four

We started going to church at Colleyville. Bro. Brown was pastor, and his wife was your teacher. She asked you what your name was, and you told her Honey Doll. She said, "Oh, what is your other name?" You said, "Honey Doll Hall." After church, she asked me what your name was. We had some good times there.

Colleyville Assembly of God was a big change for us. It felt like it was out in the country, far from the city. I'm sure it was only a ten-minute drive, but it seemed like more. There was a railroad track running alongside the road, and open fields and trees everywhere. The parking lot wasn't even paved. It was rough gravel.

Still, I was little, and those first years come in

bits and snatches to me. Songs that were sometimes too loud, images of toys I can't quite remember, and sleeping during service, oblivious to a hundred people praising God and rattling tambourines.

I would meet several lifelong friends at Colley-ville Assembly. That was later, though. That first day I think was when I suspected my real name wasn't Honey Doll. I had never imagined that before. I recall the frustration of explaining my name. Couldn't the pretty lady understand what I was saying? Honey. Doll. Hall. How much clearer could I be?

You know, sometimes people just don't understand.

When Mom and Daddy wanted to get married, their families didn't get it. Mom has told me how they were going to church together. They were both Christians. What more could anyone want? Still, Evelyn shared with my mother that there was a disturbance in the family over Mom marrying Daddy. The family didn't agree with their desire to get married. I suppose they didn't understand.

It wasn't a comfortable time, and there were probably dark looks and unwelcome snide comments. Mom says it was disheartening. She'd always felt special in her family, and now she didn't feel special anymore. One day, Evelyn and Marvin came up for a visit, and Mom decided she'd had enough. "I think I'll go home with you. I need to get away from here for a while."

She did, too. However, my first day at Colleyville Assembly, I was only four. I couldn't run away. But I knew one thing.

Honey. Doll. Hall.

It was my daddy's special name for me, and how could anyone not understand that's who I was? I understand now, but then, I felt very frustrated that Sis. Brown just didn't get it.

Chapter Thirty-five

One night in the back of the building, we had put you in a crib, since you were asleep. It was just a big metal building with curtains to separate the classes. A man came in the door and said something, and it startled me, since you were back there by yourself, and the curtains were closed. Some of the men went back there to see what was going on, but as soon as he realized he was in the wrong place, he left. So, Bro. Brown kept on preaching.

When I was about 6, we moved into our house on Topper Court. It was great. It had four bedrooms, one for each of us. I got my own room, one that I didn't have to share with anyone.

Mom tells me that when we were in Germany, we went to see the tulips in Holland. I was too young to remember, but she was impressed by the acres of flowers as far as the eye could see.

I was more impressed with a bedroom that kept other people's eyes on the far side of my door. I don't know that I'd feel so secure with a sheet of fabric forming the walls of my room.

With Steven, I've always been especially careful to keep him safe from everything I could think of. If he played outside, I was there. In the mall, I made sure I could always see or touch him. In a parking lot, I always put him in the car first, then walked around to my side. Even in public restrooms, when he was small, I took him in with me and let him use the stall while I stood guard outside.

Overprotective? I don't think so. He's a healthy, normal man today, and he's that way because I watched out for him every day of his life.

I'm glad someone came and checked on me that night. Even so, I had no cause to worry. I was a child, I had parents I trusted, and if something did happen, I knew my daddy would come out, guns blazing, to right whatever wrong had been done to me.

There's no better feeling than that, and today, Daddy might be older, and I might be grown up, but I know he would do the same for me even now.

Chapter Thirty-six

We stayed on Bonzer for about a year. They put it up for sale, and we thought it wouldn't sell since we were living there. But, in December, it sold, and we had to move. The Lord helped us to find an apartment on Belknap Street. It was so nice, with carpet and central air. We really praised the Lord for it.

After I married, Farley and I lived in a house we sold three times. The first time, the deal fell through before we could close. The second time, we closed on our house and bought another one, only to have our buyers back out before the funds could transfer. The third time, we finally closed the deal.

I'm sure my mother hoped the deal would fall through on our Bonzer Street house. However, my

Aunt Faye wanted to be certain we had a place to live, and she came to our rescue. She gave Mom information about some apartments on Belknap Street. Mom called, explained our situation, and asked if she could come see them. The manager asked if she was on the list.

"List?" my mother asked. "What sort of list?"

She had to be on a waiting list to get an apartment. The manager agreed to show her the place anyway, reminding her he didn't have one for her. My mom, however, can be very persuasive. Remember, she knows that what she wants must be in God's will, and she just asks.

The manager agreed to put her at the top of the list if she made a cash deposit, and we moved in within a few days. I was so excited, I wanted everyone who lived around us to know Jesus, and so I went around passing out tracts with Col. Sanders' picture on them. The manager eventually learned what I was doing, but by then I was out of tracts. Mom told me I couldn't pass out any more tracts. It nearly broke my heart, because I didn't want the people around us to miss out on heaven.

So, instead, I learned to swing on the monkey

bars in the playground just outside our door. I loved living there.

Thanks, Mom, for not giving up when everyone said we wouldn't be able to get an apartment in that beautiful complex.

Chapter Thirty-seven

Once when we were at Colleyville, you won a contest at church, and Sis. Brown gave you a beautiful pair of pajamas. You would always draw her pretty pictures and bring her flowers. Then Jackie Moore was your teacher, and you really loved her. She felt the same way about you.

I got to wear a crown when I won this contest. I don't really remember what it was for, scripture memorization, or collecting pennies, or something. The important thing was how it made me feel.

I felt like a true princess that day.

When Steven was 16, Mom and Dad went on an Alaskan cruise with us. We had one night in Seattle before checking in on the ship the next morning, and I'd worked out a really good deal for the Penthouse

Suite at the Sheraton. Mom didn't know. Steven wanted to surprise her, so he hid the penthouse button on the elevator. Indeed, she was surprised when the doors opened up, and we had a two-story vista of the harbor through our windows.

The next day we had a limousine pick us up at the hotel, and we took a driving tour of the city before we boarded the ship. We were celebrating both Mother's Day and my parents' wedding anniversary, and we wanted the entire trip to make them feel special.

We have pictures of Mom and Dad standing on the curving staircase aboard the ship. The glamorous interior of the ship sparkles in the background, the brass handrails gleam in the lights, and Mom is elegant in a floor-length gown and holding a sequined purse.

Sometimes it's good to feel like a princess, especially when you're the mother of one.

What did I win in that contest all those years ago? A pair of pajamas. I wore them until I wore them out. Being a princess isn't about diamonds and jewels. I learned that a long time ago. A princess becomes royalty when she feels special inside.

When I wore that crown at Colleyville Assembly, I felt like I was on a grand staircase, and the world was paying attention to me.

I became a princess that day, maybe wearing pajamas once we got home, but a princess, none-the-less.

Chapter Thirty-eight

*One Sunday, Faye asked if we wanted to go to
Seminary South for an Easter pageant for the
children. Her sister-in-law was going to take her
two girls. So, we took you. You wore a yellow dress,
and I had put your hair up on top of your head in
curls, and left a couple hanging down on the sides.
We had small flowers around the curl on top of
your head. You were in the top ten that were
chosen.*

Seminary South was the first real shopping mall to be built in Fort Worth. Today, malls are totally enclosed, with all the walkways air conditioned and heated. At Seminary South, the walkways were open air; landscaped with lush plantings, trees, and flowers; and sparkling water fountains to dip your fingers in and splash your brother when he wasn't looking.

I knew Laura and Lisa were signed up for a children's fashion show. They were in beautiful dresses, with their hair all in curls. I was there because Aunt Faye invited us, and I wanted to go. Besides, I was 6, so where Mom went, I had to tag along.

When we got there, Mom knelt down, put her hands beside my face, and told me I was getting to participate, too. Oh, no, I thought. Not me!

Yes, me. The pageant was outside, amid the trees and the flowers, with the sound of water in the background. I remember all of that. I also remember the butterflies dancing in my stomach when they called my name. I walked across the stage, and I turned around in front of all those people. I could see you out in the crowd, and I felt so proud. Everyone was paying attention to me!

I placed in the contest, and I was so happy. I hadn't expected to be in the contest at all. I wasn't dressed up, and I still got picked.

Sometimes I think of all those years ago when Daddy wanted to marry you, and you said it had to be on a Saturday, or there was no deal. Then you learned it was Halloween, and Daddy wouldn't let you change the date. He was afraid you'd change your mind. If you had, I wouldn't be standing on that stage at six years old, a princess among princesses.

I love you, Mom, every day. I want you to know that I will always love you for being the best mother in the world.

Chapter Thirty-nine

We were so proud of you that day.

Mother, you are so sweet! You've always been proud of me, and you know what? I am very proud to call you my mother.

For the prayers you've prayed for me and the encouragements given over my lifetime, thank you. Many times you've put my needs before your own, and for that, thank you.

Honey Doll

— Age 6 —

Ruby has been married to Edgar Hall 60+ years. She has lived in the United States, Germany, Turkey, and India. She has also visited Hawaii, Alaska, Canada, Mexico, Holland, Austria, Iran, Malaysia, Taiwan, London, and Singapore. She has been a retail store manager, nursery school teacher, children's counselor, missionary, motivational speaker, housewife, mother, and grand-mother.

Now retired from all except the last three, she lives with her husband in coastal North Carolina. She attends a local Church of God, enjoys Facebooking with friends and family from around the globe, and loves being around people.

To say Ruby is a people person is to underestimate how much she delights in other people. Ruby sees the good in everyone she meets, and she treats them with a love and affection that flows from her faith in Christ.

Ruby wrote this letter to her daughter, Diane, about the time Ruby's youngest grandson was born. As Diane organized her mother's things decades later, she came upon the sheaf of handwritten sentiments, and she knew she had to respond to her mother's heartfelt letter penned all those years ago.

www.ingramcontent.com/pod-product-compliance
Lightning Source LLC
Chambersburg PA
CBHW050353280326
41933CB00010BA/1445